A BAGFUL OF HAIKU –

87 IMPERFECTIONS

by

isabella mori

A Bagful of Haiku: 87 Imperfections

ISBN 978-0-9959021-0-7

Cover Photo by Isabella Mori
Author Photo by Tova Mori
Book Design by Carol Sill

For more information, please contact moritherapy@shaw.ca
www.abagfulofhaiku.com

i give this book
to the moment

Contents

Part 2

Essays on Haiku

Foreword

The haiku: those three little lines in concise syllabic patterns have inspired so many words and theories from poets and scholars. Practitioners of the art let their work speak for itself, leaving the reader to discover the perceptual immediacy in the poem. Throughout this book, Isabella Mori opens aspects of haiku to us in gradual stages, with an easy atmosphere and a light touch. Her book includes haiku she has written herself and reflections on principles of the poetic form. This combination of the experiential and the reflective is also a variation on the poetics of haiku.

Originally German-speaking, fluent in Spanish and English, Mori takes to the Japanese form with an awareness that goes beyond any particular culture nurtured by one language alone. In her hands the form leads to its essential goal: direct unmediated perception.

Mori's Vancouver haiku are not lofty or grand. That is not the haiku poetics she references. These haiku are direct refractions of everyday perceptions honed to focus on an instant of recognition.

This path strips the poetic art to its most minimal: an indicator of experience preserved as a seed through time. By example and by explication Mori encourages readers to find their own way to this perceptual refinement.

In further exploration, Mori takes us beyond the boundary of haiku as it has been previously understood, breaking with tradition to permit the emergence of entirely new forms. True always to the direct percept, these newer forms of haiku offer another take on the tradition's meaning.

She also touches upon her process of selecting which of her many haiku to include, showing how this book came about in a randomly-inspired mathematical crystallization of form and content.

In Part 1, Isabella presents a selection of her haiku, gathered in chapters around themes such as wabi sabi, perfection, and 'this'. Each grouping of haiku is prefaced by a description of the topic concept and its relationship to the common principles of haiku. The theme of each chapter in Part 1 emerged through Mori's process of assembling her selected haiku, her "87 imperfections."

In the reflections that comprise Part 2, these themes are further deepened with examples and reference to both Japanese and American haiku. Here Isabella adds further commentary on these topics, using quotes and examples from the full range of her haiku study and practice. The meaning of the work expands to reveal the depth of setting in which her own haiku are richly positioned. Her goal is not just to present her haiku, but to encourage and inspire us as readers to engage in haiku for ourselves.

The book is intended to be well-used, so the reader may refer back and forth from page to page, from one section to another. For it is not really a linear collection at all, but "a bagful of haiku."

A glance at the extensive bibliography shows the academic side of Mori's haiku exploration, but these concepts give way to the moment at the point of writing. Her haiku just as easily could have been collected without description, context or explanation. Just 87 imperfections. But that would not have engaged us in this conversation. Instead, Isabella guides us into poetic perception, inviting readers to become writers, to join in haiku writing as a social medium.

Is there a difference between Vancouver crows and Japanese crows? Vancouver rain and Japanese rain? Vancouver haiku and Japanese haiku? If it is anywhere, haiku is here and now, in Vancouver (or wherever you may be) today, not only in Japan hundreds of years ago, nor in Big Sur with the beats in the 1950's. For whether it is written in New York, Black Mountain, Tokyo, an alpine hut or a poet's basement room, the process of haiku is the same. Mori understands this.

And the difference between her Vancouver crows and the crows of Kyoto? Ask the perceiver – the one who works the delicate poetic mechanism of word, line, and form to say repeatedly in unique and specific iterations: This is, this is, this is.

Carol Sill, Vancouver, 2017

A FEW WORDS ABOUT THE STRUCTURE OF THIS BOOK

Each of the six chapters in Part 1 begins with an introductory prose text, reflecting and lightly touching on some ideas connected with the topics of haiku and imperfection. Each chapter ends with a selection of haiku I have written over the years.

Part 2 delves deeper into the ideas and topics touched on in Part 1 and links some of them to the work of present and past haiku poets and scholars, as well as others, from Plato to a marketing specialist. Often, there is direct reference to the content in Part 1. Thus, this book contains haiku, reflections on them, and then reflections on those reflections. I hope the reader will find that this slow, iterative meandering through the landscape of images, feelings and thoughts lends itself well to the deliberate nature of haiku.

Preface

Once upon a medieval time, Japanese men inclined towards poetry (and perhaps rice wine) gathered occasionally for *haikai no renga*, a style of collaborative poetry. One would start the first verse, another would link to it with the next verse, and so on, late into the night.

That is how haiku was born: as a *hokku*, the starting verse of haikai no renga. Eventually, hokku became a standalone, the men turned to competing who could produce the best hokku, and in the last decade of the 1800s, a baseball-loving poet, Masaoka Shiki, coined the word 'haiku.'

How this book was born is similar. The gathering from which this book grew was Twitter – millions of people linking millions of verses, none longer than 140 characters. I came up with *twaiku* for a tweeted haiku.

weathered leather leaves
hissing through the black-night wind.
there's fear in my heart.

This may have been my first twaiku, written in February or March of 2007. Like the haikai no renga men, I paid scant attention to dating and archiving. I just wanted to throw a poetic link or two into the twitter chain.

Over the years, this amounted to hundreds of poems and an ever-increasing interest in haiku, a fascination begun as a child, when my mother talked in reverential tones of the poet Klabund who, she claimed, managed the impossible: transpose haiku into German.

Maybe because of this early experience, I have always happily risen to the challenge of doing the supposed near possible of translating poetry. For over a decade now, I have paid no heed to the admonition that non-Japanese should not, could not, write true haiku.

I am no master of true haiku, which, some say, should still be referred to as hokku, and others say do not exist. I suspect that among the hundreds of haiku I have written only a few handfuls are stringently haiku (or hokku.) The rest are far, far from perfect.

But they are part of a chain, a line of poets making chains of bumbling, stumbling attempts to paint quick brushsketches of words that capture moments, nanoseconds, of experience: a falling leaf, the sound of snow crunching, the shape of a blossom, dew glistening on a grape.

I invite you now to become part of this chain. Read, think, dream, critique, google, tweet – join this chain of imperfect poets! Write your own haiku into the book! Yes, you will find empty pages just for you.

Right now this book-bag contains 87 of my little three-line imperfections. But why not add your own – make it 88, 97, 113! The magic is that the bag will not become heavier, only more interesting. Write on the lines, in the margins, take a marker and write right across the text!

This, my friends, is social media. When those haikai no renga guys got together, it was social media. When I came up with the idea of twaiku, it was social media. And scribbling these imperfections together, that's social media, too.

bag dangling
from an old chain, made fuller
by unknown friends

Part I

Haiku by Isabella Mori, with a few thoughts

Chapter 1

A MOMENT, FLEETING

wet camelia leaves
glitter under the streetlamps.
a tomcat runs home

Eight seconds. It takes eight seconds to read this, and read it slowly. Haiku are tiny, and they don't last long. They are the grasshoppers, the geckos of literature, and like most of them, earth-coloured, not flashy. If you don't pay attention, or don't look for them, it's as if they never happened.

Are haiku weighty enough then? 'Enough,' only makes sense compared to something. Enough of what? What is the length, the weight, the fullness, that needs to be attained, who determines the measures, and who gets to say that only that length, that fullness will do?

Haiku are not a full literary meal. They are not even a snack, at least not one by itself. It is easy to confuse haiku with amuse-bouches, those tiny bites of culinary art created to amuse and entertain the tastebuds.

first mouthful of rice
hot and fragrant … mmh … crowning
a long day of work

What makes a haiku more than amusing, and filling despite its negligible size, is its tradition and structure: the metaphorical *raku* dish it comes in, the manner in which it is served, how it was prepared, the place and company where it is enjoyed. Haiku is – can be – ceremony.

A traditional Japanese haiku has many rules to guide this ceremony. There is more than one parallel between tea ceremony and haiku, especially in the old form of haiku, or hokku, which was the first of *renga*, a chain of short poems composed by a gathering of poets.

Ichi go ichi e: "One time, one meeting" is one tenet of tea ceremony. No tea ceremony is like the other. Similarly, once we move beyond the facile 5-7-5 syllable (or, in Japanese, 'beat') rule of haiku, we come upon any number of guidelines and definitions, and many, many variations.

Haiku "contains the whole universe in 17 syllables. An implied message born from omission is vitally indispensable," says Inahata Teiko. It is "a poem recording the essence of a moment keenly perceived, in which nature is linking to human nature." This from the celebrated haiku poet Margaret Chula.

'Moment' – moments can only be fleeting, omitting, impermanent. Moments have a chance at perfection, at coming close to Plato's ideal (the thing itself, not its shadow): the brief blink of sunlight on a falling leaf, an actor's elegant gesture. Curious, then: why is impermanence seen as imperfect?

cat runs down the stairs
into the yard, now that spring
has opened the doors

chase that dragonfly
down the valley up the hill –
aaah, breathless rainbows

alone in a room
she sits. fifty-eight. shivering.
a car groans outside.

sunflowers not yet
planted but thought of tonight.
the soil smells ready

fading, the noises
draw her ears out. she listens
but the song is gone

belly full, a crow
staggers around the last bits
of lawn. no more worms.

waking up again
she cries; it's a cold, cold night.
her mother holds her

one last ragged breath
and autumn is over. snow
on quiet morning streets

washing the dishes
under the old neon lamp.
clean cup. wrinkled hands.

coat, hat, mitts come off
as the sun melts on my skin
and frost off my soul

Chapter 2

Perfection, Checkmarks, Desire

The word 'perfect' means literally 'made ('fect') through and through ('per')': hair combed over and over until there are no tangles left; bread baked to the point where the crust is brown and it sounds hollow when you knock on it; a child conceived, carried and born healthy.

I sit in Central Park on a picnic bench by the pond. It's a lovely afternoon in September. But wait – far from perfect: a big movie project is going on, and two trucks have just obstructed my view. What are trucks doing on the path by the pond?

Anger arrives. I took a while to select this spot. The trucks are ugly and noisy, and their drivers talk too loud and move on the grass as if they owned it. This is wrong, just wrong, for this park. I shouldn't have to put up with this.

Oh: now they drive away. They left behind cables and planks. I guess that's okay. Others still use their power drills and talk in the background but it doesn't bother me. Good, now I'm fine. But no – now they're using a saw. I don't like that sound. It disturbs me.

Drilling, apparently, is acceptable, but not the sound of saws. They can talk worker-talk thirty feet behind me but not fifteen in front of me. The quacking of the ducks is loud but beautiful; the noise of Boundary Road two hundred yards behind me much quieter but irritating.

Is perfection a thing of checkmarks? Cross off all the boxes, and then it's "made through and through." This definition is disappointing, not at all perfect. Ducks get a nice little black checkmark, workers with a saw an angry red cross, and the truck – the truck gets a loud buzzer.

Wrong, wrong!
This notion of perfection irks me.
As much as the truck does?

Now a toddler rides by on a trike way too big for him. Cute. He wears a blue helmet, neon blue, and that takes it over to the not-perfect side: What is that artificial colour doing in this park full of old trees and ducks and water?

Constant evaluation. Constant desire: I want this and not that, I want my life and everything around me to be like a Starbucks order: A childrens' temperature soy decaf grande latte with extra foam, and could you just give it a squirt of regular coffee? In this cup here, no, not in a paper cup.

What if I could arrange this park scene just so? Toddlers, yes, but with the right colour helmet, no trucks whatsoever, no car sounds from behind, and really, it's too cold now, and I would like the pond to be wider. More grass over here, please, and get those garbage cans out of my sight.

Maybe a billionaire lives like that. Maybe he would want, and make, this park just so, the grass combed, the sounds pitched precisely to his liking, all of it conceived and carried out according to his wishes and his alone. If this park was 'made through and through' like that, I would hate it.

"at my discretion,
haiku, you may be birthed."
oh, my arrogance!

fall leaves. sunshine.
pond lies peacefully, a mirror.
enter duck: ripples

this smell of fresh leaves:
a letter from october.
cold dew on ripe grapes.

tree branches banter
with the wind. thin, naked arms
see? reaching, dancing

heavy cloud cover
and a feeble winter sun.
that's not a fair fight

against a clear sky
geese: dark shapes, honks, flowing wings.
what a mild winter

heavy boots. slow crunch
on cold, cold snow. crick, crick, crick.
wind stings, breath freezes

not yet. the blossoms
are still hard and tight. the thorns
soft yet. hold on. wait.

grabs you by the throat,
that wild, wild spring rain, tosses
your world upside down

the line is broken,
the patterns change. equinox
blows with a new wind

hey, come down with me
to the river, watch together
the dragonflies swirl

apace with summer
waxes the moon, milky-thick
as it finds fullness

duck enters pond. thinks.
swim, dive or get out? thinks more.
"bang bang!" end of think.

crows: cultured learners.
beaks sharp as brains, thoughts never still.
this human bows, awed

Chapter 3

Imperfection, Wabi Sabi, Contrast

The more I learn about haiku, the more I realize how little I know.

Every scrap of information leads to a new door, opening a depth of arcana that my knowledge can never hope to bridge. One of its paths leads to *wabi sabi*, a Japanese concept beautifully described by Richard Powell as "nothing lasts, nothing is finished, and nothing is perfect."

The idea of neverending knowledge is nothing new, and it is all-pervading. (Googling it, I find one of the first results to be a dental technician's continuous search for information and improvement – applying, incidentally, yet another Japanese concept, *Kaizen*).

But ... and ... there is something mystical and pleasing about experiencing this neverending-ness in the context of haiku, itself intricately linked with wabi sabi. Basho, the grand master of haiku, embodied wabi sabi.

Walking on foot all by himself, his long travels through Japan must have seemed neverending sometimes, and never finished. He carried an absolute minimum number of possessions. His wanderings, I imagine, stretched along a continuum, or a circle.

Feeling free in solitude.
Cold. Lonely.
Sweet melancholy.

Originally, wabi pointed to the loneliness of living in nature. Sabi, in older Japanese the same word as 'rust,' refers to 'chill', 'lean' or 'withered.' Today, wabi sabi is often translated as 'flawed beauty.' – Do I create flawed beauty in my haiku? Or only 'flawed?'

"Today John is sad ..... and so, so very lonely ..... he's also chilly" This shows the 5-7-5 structure, includes loneliness (even melancholy?) as well as 'chill.' But, unfortunately, it is not a good haiku.

'Not good' is not the same as 'flawed.' What is a flaw? The fly in the ointment, the 3% missing from 100%, a beauty mark, a limp, a missing button? A flaw is a difference noticed on a whole. John's haiku is boring, clichéd, not cohesive, unskillful. It may be flawed, but it is not flawed beauty.

Perhaps John's haiku needs a kireji, the 'cutting' element that some say is mandatory for a haiku. A kireji 'cuts', or contrasts, splits, separates one part of the haiku from the other. It's as if one takes a surprised or shocked little breath:

the crow wasn't prepared
but there it sat, all that garbage.
oh my! delicious!

We don't know what the crow wasn't prepared for – ah: 'but' it is an unusual quantity of garbage. 'Oh my' leads to the coupling of 'delicious' and 'garbage', something that for humans shows quite a contrast.

Where does the beauty lie? In the crow? The deliciousness? Could we take it further and see beauty in the garbage, the shapes and colours, the fabulousness of chaos? And the sharp intake of breath, does it come from the contrast? From the invitation to look at garbage in a different way?

i guess i'll wait here
on this street corner for spring
to arrive. cold feet.

getting short on light
these november days. red sun
long before dinner

chinese guy, biking
down my street. no gloves.
i watch, my house warm

twelve broken lanterns
on a rainy, slippery bridge.
soft-light quiver

grass all torn up
crows sure love to peck out lawn bugs.
looks like a war zone

trembling in the wind
stands a lone faded flower
that forgot to wilt

the sound of snow falls
on her tired, old ears
and lingers, lingers ...

i misunderstand
these winter days when i stay
huddled in my cave

drags himself on legs
frail from twelve years of chasing
after cats: old dog

alarm digs into
my dreams and i abandon
my sweet pillow.

lend me your flashlight
said the grim reaper. his eyes
had gone dim. old age.

Chapter 4

Not Wabi Sabi: Exclamations, violence and harsh awakenings

One element of wabi sabi is mutedness, understatement. Imagine Queen Elizabeth II in her wellingtons, quietly trudging through the forest with her dogs. That is wabi sabi. Now imagine Cher on stage, bright lipstick, made up to the hilt, belting out "Believe". Not wabi sabi.

What, though, if the flawed, muted beauty of wabi sabi repeats without pause? What if the Queen's forest were endless, never interrupted by a highway or a gaggle of loudmouthed teenage girls? We would be back to the Monopoly Man's ideal park – beautiful. And frozen.

Despite the flaws and brokenness associated with wabi sabi, a drive for purity in haiku allures me – and almost mocks me to break it. And! And! This mocking is part of my haikuing. A circle.

sooner than i want
come the fog and the dry leaves
oh goodbye summer

This would be an example of a 'pure' English haiku. 5-7-5 syllables, the middle line visibly longer than the first and last, no punctuation, a cutting word ('oh'), contrast, seasons, the absence of interpretation and/or obvious human thoughts or emotions, and the melancholy of wabi sabi. But:

we left him behind,
that sinister man, harper.
cheers and relief!!!!

This haiku fell out of me, uncontrolled, unstructured, defying most purist rules, and look, not only does it contain punctuation but an exclamation mark – gauche for a haiku – oh no, four of them!!!! "Don't call it a haiku, call it a short poem," a voice whispers, but I don't want to heed it.

Those exclamation marks. They're the harlot-red lipstick of haiku. Indiscreet like politics, and un-melancholic: 'cheers' and 'relief.' But what can I do? I am not a zen statue, I'm a human, my flaws are not always beautiful, I'm riddled with emotions and addicted to potatoes. Exclamation mark!

Exclamation marks are loud, and noise is – can be – a form of violence. Beating is violent, lies, even rollercoasters are violent. Death and war are violence. Queen Elizabeth, haikuing, ambling through Essex, would never mention violence.

Are these haiku too loud?
Too enamoured with the human experience?
Do they need to put on their wellies again, return to the autumn-wet forest?

"enough with your lies!"
he yearned for sun, not shadows
and yanked the curtains

pearls of red blood drip
from the beak of this pigeon.
oh, so many cars

addiction: lust "must"
never "maybe" or "later"
and wants THIS and NOW

"i deserve! deserve!"
she screamed. her dog hid under
the bed, embarrassed

"you choose!" "no, no, you!"
endless babble, round and round.
god watches and snorts

she became extinct
that's what she felt, after yet
another beating

yes, i like staring.
people are so interesting!
hands! eyebrows! noses!

"filth" a word that spews
emotions, makes us recoil.
it needs compassion.

really. believe me.
yes, this is for your own good.
WHACK! and one more blow

hey hey hey, hay moon!
move over! turn your light down.
it's time to ease off

rollercoaster ride:
fear! joy! pain! love! up, down, down
up, down. trickster laughs.

dominated by
addiction, over'n over
she click-clicks the mouse

the prize is nothing.
bursting-seams nothing, smiling
a tiny, full smile

wait! you haven't seen yet
what the sun can do! wait!
spring is almost here!

Chapter 5

This. No more.

This is.

The melody of those words remains hanging, unresolved; it feels like an incomplete sentence. There is a sense of discomfort, of "ok, say it, what is it?" We want sentences like 'this is brown, and it is brown because ...' or 'this is brown and I approve.'

'This is' is hard to bear; 'this is brown / white / soft / immense' is a little better, but not much. "And ...?" goes the insistent mind, "Why are you telling me? Why should I care? Why should I spend time on such common words?"

There is no should. You don't have to spend time, you don't have to care – but also, there is no need for explanation, evaluation, or hurrying on. This winter light as it glints off the roof just is. This tea drinking just is.

And this watching, tasting, listening, feeling, smelling, touching, thinking, this doing and not-doing, this glancing at a few words just is, and you don't have to worry that it will go on is-ing forever because any second now the sun will move, the tea cup will empty.

come sit for a while
on this wooden bench with me
stare into the moon

In the meantime, in this moment now, this is. 'This' points: this bench, this mountain, this rain. Not all benches, not the idea of rain, not mountains as a concept – no, no, this one, here, as it appears, as its gestalt arises right now, right before us: this tulip blossom.

And it *is*. Perhaps just for a moment or for a few days, but doubtless this phenomenon right before us is. In this very moment it exists, conveying a taste of the universal I AM of pure awareness, devoid of perceptions, associations or memories.

curving around
a shape imagined by god:
tulip blossoms

But just a taste; maybe less: like the lingering feeling after a vivid dream, almost tangible but imageless, wordless. Yet, still, haiku tries to capture in a poetic net that is-ness and this-ness when time, space and matter come together in the illumination of a moment.

Never successful, though:

Ever tried. ever failed.
No matter. try again.
Fail again. fail better.

Samuel Beckett wrote this, not as a haiku, but as his attempt to arrange words in such a way as to say, *this*. This multi-layered, complex, four, five, six-dimensional experience. Maybe we can call some words into the void and, hearing an echo, understand better?

up on the 12th floor
hair black, voice soft as velvet
echo is her name

seven coyotes
this april dream-night. crows
asleep, fearless

soft pillow, soft breath;
he sleeps already. i'm up
drinking tea. midnight.

longer and longer
it takes for the sun to drown
in the pacific

immense yellow ball
rolling up the horizon:
sweet buttery light

"i choose clouds, rain, snow"
said december. close my doors
i did. lit a fire

bent from old old age
this gnarly oak lives on.
a big bird house

winter sunlight
shining down, softly, on my
neighbour's white house

out of the soil,
wet, peeks a dew worm.
earth mover.

snow makes no effort,
slays no dragons, just blankets
the mountains, softly

low, down by the lake,
a swan dreams about mating,
her feathers bride-white

Chapter 6

A Bag Full

A woman's purse: Notes from a library session on poetry, hand cream, a book (Melody Beatty on codependence), emergency pantyhose, a key chain with a beat-up tiny teddy bear on it, a dog-eared photograph of a house with a mossy roof.

Sleeping pills,
an eye shade from the last plane trip,
and crumbs, origin unknown.

There is no order to it. Or: there is order to it only in a very chaotic way. Chaos in the ordinary sense, and chaos as it is used in chaos theory. I tumble back and forth between delighting in chaotic unpredictability and trying to understand its patterns.

looks like waste, don't it
worms, leaves, dirt in the backyard.
full-of-life compost

At the same time, I am reminded of the Swiss artist Ursus Wehrli who took to tidying up art, van Gogh's *Bedroom in Arles*, for example: he stacked all the furniture on the bed and stowed the rest under the bed. No more chaos in van Gogh's paintings!

Let's try it with this haiku:

zip? no, it does not
it moves like an old turtle
slow, in november

How about an alphabetical version?

an does in it it
like moves no not november
old slow turtle zip

Or ordered by length of word:

an in it it no
not old zip does like slow
moves turtle november

These order-examples produce chaos. "Those are the wrong kinds of order!" you might say – but what is the right one? We could also take the content and tidy it up grammatically so that the 'meaning' stays the same and all nonsense is removed:

it does not zip
it moves slowly, like a turtle
in november.

"No, no," you say, "just because it has a 5-7-5 form (and barely at that), it doesn't sound like a haiku and is boring and pointless." Take out the chaos and that element of the almost-accidental that we find in most haiku, and the magic disappears.

Without that magic, we can easily slip into interpretation, rather than the quietly reflective, contemplative mode so much better suited to haiku. We might poke and prod and look for certainty about what 'it' is, for example, or what is 'meant' by the poem.

Like the crumbs in the old purse and the long-forgotten reason why that teddy bear came to hang from the keychain, the meaning of the haiku might not be easy to decipher, and there might be more than one meaning.

But it still hangs together: it still all came together in this very purse belonging to this very person. Still some mysterious process converged in placing the 'zip' precisely into this haiku with a turtle in November.

In the bag of this chapter you find codependence, Bob Marley, yawns, fingertips, staring, Old Smith, blood, comrades, bras, warm socks, a teddy bear, up North, dreams and blue faces. No rhyme. No reason. Make you own sense of it. Put it into your bag. Hang a haiku from your keychain.

codependence
slithers along pink heart-shaped
trails towards my core

discreet and quiet
are his yawns. his hands tremble
and his eyes are old

my hands know poems
better than my head. i rely
on my fingertips

roof green from moss
grown over twelve neglected years -
old smith, he's long dead

tiny tracks of blood:
vessels, bursting, crack his eyes.
lids close. thoughts escape.

your wish is my - uh
comrade? what was it again?
or quicksand? darn it

my cup runneth o'er
she said, sighed, and proceeded
to buy a new bra

"nice" – it's bland, they say.
to me, though, it feels comfy
a soft, warm-sock word

that ol' prospector
up in the frozen, dark north
still mumbles and digs

three in the morning.
soft feathers in my pillow,
and violent dreams

anxious mcgregor
sits on his horse, afearin'
blue faces. hates war.

often, after work
she stares at her fingernails
devoid of feeling

fifty-eight and still
i play at being an adult.
my teddybear smiles

marley fill i heart
with rasta beat of justice.
pray i follow jah

Part 2

Essays on Haiku

The word 'essay' means to attempt. The following contains attempts to delve further into the world of haiku, expanding on concepts touched on in Part 1, with examples from Japanese and English-language poets.

Reflections on Chapter I – A Moment, Fleeting

Moments and breath

What is a haiku? Some say: a one-breath poem. Naomi Wakan is more precise: "It can be recited between an in-breath and an out-breath."

And here I am, writing pages and pages about it ...

Are haiku weighty enough then? 'Enough' only makes sense compared to something. Enough of what?

How about weighty enough compared to breath? Breathing in and out in the eight seconds or less it takes to slowly read a haiku is comfortable. Even breathing out in eight seconds so one can speak the haiku aloud is not an imposition.

Koans and Zen

"How much does a breath weigh?"seems like a koan. A koan is an utterance, often a riddle-type question set to provoke a zen student into abandoning old ways of thinking and perceiving.

Sometimes haiku can sound like a koan:

even stones in streams
of mountain water compose
songs to wild cherries

(Soseki, trans. Beilenson/Behn)

How are haiku and Zen connected? This question is often asked. Much of it has something to do with Basho's deep devotion to Zen, as well as the most influential translator of haiku, R.H. Blyth, a strong proponent of haiku's zen aspects. The connection between zen and haiku strengthened even further with the beat poets Gary Snyder and Jack Kerouac, who rooted haiku into American poetics. Both men had a strong connection with zen.

Also, many zen practitioners deepen their practice with haiku. The tradition of writing haiku from a spontaneous and purely observational point of view is very similar to the zen – and Buddhist – idea that enlightenment comes from ridding ourselves of all the perceptual filters that stand between us and reality. In this approach, the batting of a crow's wing is just that, not something similar to the sound of a helicopter, or a metaphor for darkness leaving, or an annoying sound – no, it is only flap, flap, flap.

All this is true, and also true for me: I experience a strong connection between haiku and my Buddhist leanings. However, I would be mistaken to state that there must be a direct connection between zen and haiku. Haiku translators and poets Bill Higginson and Penny Harter draw an interesting parallel between haiku and European art. They say it is impossible to imagine any form of European art without the context and vast cultural background of Christianity; however, it makes no sense to think of European art as Christian art. Just so with haiku and zen.

Is haiku a spiritual or an aesthetic experience? This question seems rather un-zen to me. Zen, and many other expressions of Buddhism, tries to be as close as possible to reality, that-which-is. Spirituality and religion are concepts, ideas made up by humans. Moments of love, wonder, awe, connection are real, but packaging them all into spirituality is not. This packaging is useful for certain purposes but it has no important place in either zen or haiku. That does not mean it does not crop up here and there, as in Kawabata Bosha's haiku

spring night
in bed, i long for
kuanyin

haru-no yo ya nereba koishiki kanzeon (trans. Ueda; my adaptation)

Kanzeon (also known as Kuanyin) is a Boddhisattva who personifies compassion, mercy and gentleness. Bodhisattvas are enlightened beings who have made a vow not to enter heaven until every last sentient being is free from suffering.

And ... but ... (paradoxes being such a zen *and* haiku thing)

washed at birth
washed at death -
nonsense-babble

tarai kara tarai ni utsuru chinpunkan (attributed to Issa; my adaptation)

While this haiku sounds Buddhist-inspired – Issa, if indeed the author of this haiku, was a lay priest of Pure Land Buddhism – it points out the 'nonsense-babble' (*chinpunkan*) of the analytical obsession with separating this from that. Haiku, true to life, is *neither* spiritual nor aesthetic, while at the same time *both* spiritual and aesthetic. It presents all in the moment, where concepts and definitions are irrelevant.

the singing of the birds
louder and louder, then softer and softer
to silence

saezuri no takamari owari shizumarinu (Kyoshi, trans. Blyth)

Tradition and Structure

In true paradoxical fashion, let's go from one end to the other: From silence to what could be seen as the nonsensical babble of definitions and structure:

> *What makes a haiku more than amusing, and filling despite its negligible size? It is its tradition and structure: the metaphorical raku dish it comes in, the manner in which it is served, how it was prepared, the place and company where it is enjoyed. Haiku is – can be – ceremony.*
>
> *A traditional Japanese haiku follows many rules to guide this ceremony.*

In fact, there are so many rules, some of them contradictory, that it is understandable that Henderson, the early translator who advocated an aesthetic approach to haiku, suggested American writers of haiku should figure out their own standards. Hendersen felt, however, that this should be done on a foundation of grasping at least some of the rules and structures underlying the work of Japanese writers over the centuries. Let us look at some of these rules.

Short: Lines, syllables, and a brief moment

A typical non-Japanese haiku has three lines. The typical Japanese haiku is written in one vertical line but its grammatical structure is such that it usually indicates three sections. Not-so-typical Western haiku have one, two, three, four, five lines – or more. I have seen haiku with one word per line.

Then there are those syllables. Neither English nor Japanese are easy to funnel into these little language-organizing units we commonly understand as syllables. The word water is simple enough: two syllables, 'wa' - and - 'ter.' But look at the word 'mirror': mir-ror? mirr-or? What if you pronounce it something like 'meer' or 'mirr'? It is often not obvious whether a poem is meant to be read on the page, out loud by the reader with her or his own pronunciation habits, or out loud imagining how the writer might have pronounced it. The question of syllables, and therefore meter, is of particular interest in a form like haiku, where rhythm plays a central role. As an aside, many haiku experts argue that we should not even talk about syllables but rather morae or beats (*on*), linguistic units that in a language like Japanese determine where a word is stressed.

I first thought Japanese was as easy as the other two languages I am intimately familiar with. German and Spanish are clear cut when it comes to syllables. Easy, then: Su-shi. Sa-shi-mi. But it turns out it is complicated in ways hard to understand for non-Japanese. The sound/letter 'n', for example, is its own syllable or *on*. How long a vowel is also comes into play. The word 'Tokyo' (pronounced Tohkyoh) has two long vowels and therefore four *on*: To-o-kyo-o.

Gilbert and Yoneoka tell us that Henderson wrote 'the rigid 17-syllable requirement . . . does not exist in Japan . . . and who started it for English syllables I do not know.' On the other hand, Yasuda makes a passionate claim that the 5-7-5 structure as we know it makes possible a perception of balance, harmony and symmetry. Should you read the chapter *Five-Seven-Five* in *The Japanese Haiku*, you may be better able to follow his reasoning than I. I propose that it does not matter much. The 5-7-5 structure is so well established and creates such a useful form that even the woolliest reasons to substantiate it do not undermine its poetic practicality. And with that established practicality comes magic: even a four-line, thirteen-syllable poem can lay claim to being a haiku:

late at night
a sliding door
in the distance
is closed

yonaka-no fusuma toku shimeraretaru (Hosai, trans. Ueda)

It is as if this unruly haiku still grows on a trellis of the 5-7-5 structure.

We still have brevity of content, and it is the brevity that lends so much richness to this haiku. Making it longer or filling it up would turn this word-image into boring nonsense, or, at the very least, would take the magic away. Part of this magic comes from the connection between the word-image and our own individual, private experiences. For example, I experience a distinctive sound-feeling when most people have gone to sleep and I am one of the few left awake. The sound of a sliding door closing in the distance at 1:30 in the morning is very, very different from the sound of that same door twelve hours later – if I can hear it at all then. However, all that wordiness I produced just now is unpoetic and un-special compared to Hosai's haiku. Lightly, briefly, quietly, it points to that moment, that night, that door, and I am touched. These eleven words (only four in Japanese!) take me into the depth of an interesting, special, poetic breath-long moment. As stated earlier:

Haiku contains the whole universe in 17 syllables.

Nature and seasons

I go on to cite Margaret Chula, that a haiku is

> *a poem recording the essence of a moment keenly perceived, in which nature is linking to human nature.*

That definition would probably please Henderson, whose opinion was that haiku are "concerned with human emotions." That not everyone agrees has by now been amply shown. But haiku are concerned with nature in the widest sense. They touch on what can be felt at the core of a thing, idea or organism:

belly full, a crow
staggers around the last bits
of lawn. no more worms.

This haiku refers to a quintessential Vancouver sight: crows digging up lawns until there is hardly anything left – no more worms but also no more lawn. A simple moment in nature. Then there is the nature of human experience:

waking up again
she cries; it's a cold, cold night.
her mother holds her

This is a moment in my life, encapsulating one of the many nights our youngest daughter woke up from a nightmare. It was not just the temperature that was cold but our young one's terrifying dreams, and like any terrified human being, she needed the warmth of a familiar body and loving embrace.

How about Jack Kerouac –

> hot coffee
> and a cigarette –
> who needs zazen?

Sitting in zen meditation is called *zazen*. Experiencing it can be mentally, emotionally and physically uncomfortable if not outright painful, and this, too, is part of the nature of zazen. Juxtaposed we have the nature of sitting down for coffee and a cigarette. We are left to ponder the connection. There is something essential, nature-al, about the coffee and cigarette on the one hand and zazen on the other, sitting side-by side in this haiku.

The first two haiku point, at least vaguely, to a season. The first is probably not in the winter, the second probably not in the summer. In traditional Japanese haiku, including season is anything but vague – there are long lists of acceptable or prescribed *kigo*, or season words. Spring rain, or *harusame*, is one of them. Season words carry specific cultural contexts which may be one reason kigo is sometimes referred to as the 'marrow' of a haiku. In the West, we have few of these culturally shared seasons, (Christmas and the New Year perhaps are exceptions.) To find the season, we need to dig deeper and wider. The belly-full crows evoke gardening season, but also adulthood (baby crows cannot peck out those worms yet) and the cycle of life and death: dead worms and torn-up grass roots mean well-fed crows.

Taking the approach of cycles also works for Kerouac's haiku which at first glance looks devoid of seasons. I already used the metaphor of on the one hand, and on the other above; there is a weighing up, almost like on a teeter-totter. Is the zazen higher now, or coffee and cigarettes? Is enlightenment reached when they can be held in balance?

Here, then, are the elements that, to my imperfect understanding, make a short poem a haiku: Extreme brevity in form and content, often of three-line length, and personally experienced sense-content that reflects the essential or cyclical nature of life.

There is something more than technical to this, otherwise what we are looking at here is just intellectual navelgazing, the antithesis of haiku. This 'something more' can be expressed poetically ....

a small black seed
held up, finger to thumb –
irises next year

We will have to come back to this 'something more.' So much easier to talk about structure and rules.

Structure, rules – a long list

Here are most of the rules or guidelines I have found while studying haiku:

A 5-7-5 structure
Line two is longer than lines one and three
A 2-3-2 beat (stress) structure, e.g.

WASHing the DISHes
under the OLD NEon LAMP.
clean CUP. wrinkled HANDS.

Presents rather than describes an image
Shows an image; preferably a concrete one
Two images are illuminated by a third

Not intellectual or obscure
Virtually free of concepts, metaphors and similes
Avoids sentimentality and clichés

Does not mention emotions, only evokes them
The haiku needs to come to the writer, it is never written on demand
Created from direct personal experience

Arises from a stance of humility and sincerity
Composed in an attitude of contemplation and absorption
Not written when the poet is overcome by emotion

Contains a contrast, comparison or paradox
Something is omitted; the part suggests the whole
Shows more than one sensory modality

Uses plain, unpretentious language
Has few or no pronouns (I, you, etc.) and articles (a, the)
Is in present tense

No punctuation
Written in all lower case
No full sentences

Does not rhyme
Almost devoid of adjectives (e.g. blue, large) and adverbs (-ly words such as quickly)
Free of gerunds (-ing words)

As close to Japanese haiku ideals as possible
Is only a haiku if it follows the haiku 'recipe,' the way a scone is only a scone if it follows a scone recipe.
To be written only by people deeply familiar with Japanese language and culture

Has only one kireji
Alludes to wabi, or sabi, or wabi sabi
Needs a 'season word' (kigo)

Evokes feelings without mentioning the emotion
Pays attention to rhythm but is not iambic or anapestic
Makes the reader think

Sounds as lovely spoken as read on the page
So incisive that it can be almost immediately memorized
Can be said in one breath

Has no title / Can have a title
Composed of two major parts of varying lengths, such as 5-12, 12-5
Should not exceed 17 syllables

Mentions natural elements
Describes common, everyday occurrences
About a single happening or moment

Not written from the imagination or memory
Shows "growth" (Henderson): more emotion is perceived with repeated reading
No anthropomorphism

Has a where, a what and a when
Is clearly different from a *hokku*, a *senryu* and a *waka*
Contains no "poetic trickery" (Kerouac)

Contrasts permanence and impermanence
Aspires to *yugen,* a subtle profoundness capturing the essence of what is described in the haiku
Seeks out new and revealing perspectives on the human and physical condition

More moments

Yes, it is easier to talk about rules. Obligingly, they stand still, can be named, listed, ordered. Moments, on the other hand –

> *... can only be fleeting, impermanent. Moments have a chance at perfection, at coming close to Plato's ideal (the thing itself, not its shadow): the brief blink of sunlight on a falling leaf, an actor's elegant gesture.*

Moments do not stand still. Possibly, the only hope we ever have of capturing the moment is in art. The challenge is that moments are embedded in vast worlds of context.

one last ragged breath
and autumn is over. snow
on quiet morning streets

In the *Shurangama Sutra* the Buddha talks about not mistaking the finger pointing at the moon for the moon. Many creative works such as haiku are, in the end, just pointing fingers. Nevertheless, haiku do 'have a chance' at least of somewhat accurately painting, capturing, pointing a finger at the moment as well as at its context. Even a simple image of early winter is embedded in layers of context. Those who have never lived with the change from fall to the last season might find abstract enjoyment in this haiku but they would not know the particular soundscape to which it refers and that feeling of – well, what is it? Awe? Surprise? – that comes with noticing those first few snow-covered hours.

Creative works such as haiku 'have a chance' not only of accurately painting, capturing, pointing a finger at the moment but also at its context. Success is not guaranteed, not by any means. I daresay even van Gogh did not manage to one hundred percent accurately portray the Platonic reality of a night full of stars; how much less an apprentice haiku poet such as I. But there is something fierce and mystical about the desire that drives van Gogh, and me, Bach, and the drama teacher at your local high school, Picasso and, yes, even Danielle Steel, the romance writer, to consistently point (and wag, and shake) our fingers at the moon of the moment and the vast sky-context around it. Some magical element there makes the creative act work, sometimes sort of, sometimes magnificently. We come back for more, and if the stars align, our audience does, too.

Impermanence and Imperfection

Curious, then: why is impermanence seen as imperfect?

Why indeed?

Aah, because permanence is such a lovely illusion: 'And they lived happily ever after.' Perfection, at least in one of its forms, is a dream. We imagine the princess and the prince, holding hands, walking on a gilded, rose-strewn path that goes on and on and on. Most of us do not stay with this image for longer than it takes to read these last few words. There it is, tucked away, our image of forever-ever-after. Perfect. A sense of relief comes, phew, at least there is something we can rely on, this one will not turn out bad, this one will stay beautiful and loving and sweet-smelling forever.

As humans, we need these little tucked-away corners of illusion, places we can rest on without them wriggling away under us or turning into fire-spewing, jackhammer-roaring dragons. Life is hard and we need soft places.

This is where we can say hello to the Buddha again, the Gautama who never wholly disappears from haiku. (Or maybe it is Amidha Buddha, the Buddha of the Japanese Pure Land Buddhism.) The Buddha would say that hiding away on those soft places of illusion ultimately makes life even harder. The confrontation and discrepancy with everyday reality is just too stark. That resting place we imagine in perfection can only be found in living with reality exactly as it is, moment by moment. Impermanence is one of the absolute conditions of life; we need to embrace it, not freeze it in manufactured images of some elusive 'forever.'

Reflections on Chapter 2 – Perfection, Checkmarks, Desire

Imperfection, anger, certainty

Anger arrives. It took me a while to select this spot. The trucks are ugly and noisy, and the workers who drive talk too loud and move on the grass as if they owned it. This is wrong, just wrong, for this park. I shouldn't have to put up with this.

Oh: now they drive away. They left some cables and planks. I guess that's okay. Others are still drilling and talking in the background but it doesn't bother me. Good, now I'm fine. But no now they're using a saw. I don't like that sound. It disturbs me.

More imperfection: Anger and certainty ("this is wrong, just wrong") flitting quickly to "I guess that's okay" to "but no." Mood, certainty, righteousness, acceptance, criticism: all are unsteady, fleeting images on a much larger canvas. What that canvas is, I don't know. The 'True Self?' I am suspicious of such a grand scheme.

Is perfection a matter of checkmarks? Cross off all the boxes, and it's made perfect through and through. This definition is disappointing, not at all perfect. Ducks get a nice little black checkmark, workers with a saw get an angry red cross, and the truck – the truck gets a loud buzzer.

Wrong, wrong!
This notion of perfection irks me.
As much as the truck does?

...What if I could arrange this park scene just so? Toddlers, yes, but with the right colour helmet, no trucks whatsoever, no car sounds from behind, and really, it's a bit too cold now, and I would probably like the pond to be wider. More grass over here, please, and get those garbage cans out of my sight.

... If this park were 'made through and through' like that, I would hate it.

On an intuitive level it makes sense; there is something artificial and willful about perfections that come about through meeting a set of predetermined criteria – ticking off the boxes. And one could say, well, that's what makes perfection so undesirable. But could a perfection really be that undesirable? Would it still be a perfection?

Desire, individuality

Maybe perfection is about desire: when nothing is left to desire, there is perfection. Aaah, this cup of tea is perfect. All my tea-desires have been met, quenched. This view makes perfection rooted in time and individuality. Tomorrow the tea-desire may return and collide with a lukewarm, tasteless brew. Or, while I have had my tea-desire fulfilled many times, perhaps you have never found that pleasure. Nothing we can say about 'tea' or even very specifically, 'Decaf Earl Grey' could universally be called perfect.

And if perfection is rooted in time and individuality, is it still perfection?

Correctness

tree branches banter
with the wind. thin, naked arms
see? reaching, dancing

Quite correct, this haiku:

It has an allusion to season – 'naked tree branches'(1). We have a clear 5-7-5 syllable structure with none of those English words that make one wonder how many syllables it has (fire and mirror, for example.) (2) A kireji or 'cutting word' makes us pause: "see?" (3) The haiku occurs in nature (4), captures a fleeting image (5), and is free of any overt philosophizing (6). The language is clear and unpretentious (7).

But it is far from perfect. Six punctuation marks, for example: is that too much? James Hackett compares punctuation to an excess of jewellery: "If haiku is like a finger pointing to the moon, you don't want any jewels on the finger to distract readers from seeing the moon."

The moon would be the image, the haiku the finger – but here it becomes interesting because the finger-moon combination is itself an image. What does the moon look like? A perfect round, yellow cartoon moon? A faint sickle? Does it appear in a dark sky, accompanied by stars?

Then there is the finger, with or without jewellery, and myriad ways of showing and perceiving it. How we each represent it in our own private imagination, and how we think and feel about this representation will determine our reaction to any finger, any jewellery. It all depends on a complex tangle – or shall we say dance? – of personal experience, upbringing, current status in the world, education ...

For instance, I imagine right now the finger to be of an ex-coworker who wouldn't be caught dead without rings on her finger. She was articulate, eccentric, effusively creative, passionate, full of breath-stopping travel anecdotes. I see her finger here in my inner field of vision. It is intrusive and at the same time instructive and a propos.

The haiku about the tree branches is not perfect. Yes, yes, there may well be too much jewellery, too much interjection, not just the image itself. But here it is. This is what I saw. So I write it down.

The poems in this section try to capture all the seasons. The one above thinks of fall. And we have the others:

heavy boots. slow crunch
on cold, cold snow. crick, crick, crick.
wind stings, breath freezes

not yet. the blossoms
are still hard and tight. the thorns
soft yet. hold on. wait.

apace with summer
waxes the moon, milky-thick
as it finds fullness

Seasons aren't correct. They aren't perfect. But how our minds love to go there! A white Christmas, Easter full of daffodils, summer at the beach, fall an orderly three-month succession from crisp mornings to golden leaves to warm jackets in November. Once again, there is this schema and expectation of perfection – it should be so, and not otherwise! But the seasons just do what they want. (I am writing this during the coolest July I've ever seen in Vancouver.) Climate and weather don't care what we think and how we evaluate. Just as they are not in the category of things that can be correct or perfect, they are also not in the category of things that care. As a human being, I can only experience, react, respond, witness. Listen: this snow-sound, touch: this rosebud, look: this summer moon.

Reflections on Chapter 3 – Imperfection, Wabi Sabi, Contrast

Order into the Wabi Sabi!

Something must be revealed: just because I make such a point of my inability to produce perfection, don't let yourself be seduced into thinking I don't chase after it. Like the Swiss artist Ursus Wehrli mentioned earlier, I try, teeth gnashing, tongue sticking out, brow deeply furrowed, to wrench as much order from what fascinates and bewilders me. From some of it, at least. Wabi sabi is one example. I gathered texts about it, sifted through necessary words and phrases and not so necessary ones. Discarded the latter. Made bullet lists. Categorized, counted, recategorized. Then this cluster of concepts emerged:

Cyclical; impermanent; unpredictable; transient; transcendent; nothing lasts, nothing is finished, nothing is perfect; coming from; flow; remote; returning to; spacious.

I saw these ideas as embodying movement, or, what I called 'nonlinear time and space.' Oh, how perfectly I wished to grasp this – this thing, this idea, this *je-ne-sais-quoi* called wabi sabi!

Order all around

Putting together this book was a similar process. How to sift through hundreds of haiku? Endless, endless categorization. The easiest part was to delete those that never would be good enough, like this one:

april rain beats
down on skylight, wind howls
awesome

Once I settled on an acceptable selection, it occurred to me to ask potential readers to rate them. Creating a survey seemed to be a good idea – but which haiku to use? If the survey only included those haiku I liked it would only confirm my own biases – but which of the not-so-great ones to include? This one received favorable ratings:

mom's old age rings loud
in my ears. i fight sadness.
should i surrender?

I decided against that one, too. At the moment of selection, I felt it contained too many feelings, too much reflection, and was too simplistic.

The survey was just the beginning. Once my selection was reduced to 150, I printed everything and cut out each haiku, creating little haiku-snippets. That turned out to be a much better method than my original idea of ordering them all on a spreadsheet.

After the snipping, more categorization! Was this about nature? Was there a season word? Did it contain a sense of surprise or contrast, a 'cutting word?' Did it carry a simple idea or many? Was it humorous, did it contain animals, was it about feelings?

All together, twenty-one categories emerged. One category was about how many categories a haiku fell into! I rated the degree to which a haiku fell into each category. I spent considerable time musing over haiku with high numbers, like this one:

getting short on light
these november days. red sun
long before dinner

To wit, 5 categories with high ratings: Nature (a rating of 5), Season (10), Fall (10), Image/Visual (7), Sun/Moon/Stars/Light (8).

All this ordering was far from perfect but it helped give this book shape. Each snippet turned into a near alchemical ticket, a talisman of obscure scribbles. It was fun: I enjoyed physically handling these haiku, interacting with them, moving them around. The snippets had to have a safe home – so they ended up in ziplog bags I carried around for months in a flower-covered little gift tote. This gave me the title of the book: "A bagful of haiku."

Neverending: Kaizen

Every scrap of information leads to a new door, opening an abyss of arcana that my knowledge can never hope to plumb. One of its paths leads to wabi sabi, a Japanese concept beautifully described by Richard Powell as "nothing lasts, nothing is finished, and nothing is perfect."

The idea of neverending knowledge is all-pervading (Googling it, I find one of the first results to be a dental technician's continuous search for knowledge and improvement – applying, incidentally, yet another Japanese concept, Kaizen).

Kaizen is a Japanese business philosophy of continuous improvement. Interestingly, 'kaizen and haiku' produced 24,000 results on Google – clearly, a few other people are thinking about the connection. For example, Maggie Millard wrote:

never enough time
to make everything perfect
but better will do

It's amusing that Kaizen was born out of US post-WWII desires to find ways to easily and rapidly improve production. My haiku are North American, built on a Japanese tradition, and the Japanese concept of Kaizen came from the US.

However ... and ... there is something mystical and pleasing about experiencing this neverending-ness in haiku, itself intricately linked with wabi sabi.

Let's linger at this 'however ... and ....' for a moment. It feels important, but in a slippery way. Mystical, perhaps. 'However' implies a contradiction, 'and' points to affirmation. What do we have here? How about: These "scraps of new information" represent continuous waves of new knowledge, waves that will not last yet will not be finished. But isn't that which does not last eventually finished? Well, perhaps not. 'Waves' may be a good metaphor here. Each wave does not last long, but the process of waves arriving over and over on the shore never finishes, just ebbs, returns, ebbs, returns. Yes: mystical and pleasing. Like the waves, I will keep learning about haiku, and what I know will never be perfect. Who knows: staying mindful of that, and pointing it out the way a raku potter accentuates the cracks in her bowl, can imbue my attempts with more wabi sabi. I can keep exploring the landscape of haiku the way Basho explored Japan. Like this?

autumn twilight road
made only for the passing
of lonely men

(Basho, trans. Cohen)

Kireji

What is kireji, the 'cutting word'? Is it like the crack in the bowl? In the essays, I portray it as the surprised little breath, or a contrast. Higginson calls it a "sounded punctuation," Wakan and Yasuda refer to it as a pause ("thought pause," says Yasuda.)

Not all my haiku have kireji or thought pauses. This one, for example. It is also a complete sentence, something Reichhold frowns upon in haiku:

trembling in the wind
stands a lone faded flower
that forgot to wilt

Then again one could say this whole haiku is about a pause.

This one, on the other hand, has a colon, a punctuation often recognized as an acceptable translation or substitute for a kireji.

drags himself on legs
frail from twelve years of chasing
after cats: old dog

Correctly speaking, a kireji is not a cutting word, but a cutting word fragment (a bit like a prefix such as de- or suffix such as –esque in English). The precise translation is 'cutting letters.' It is difficult to translate or emulate kireji. Colons (:), semicolons (;), ellipses (…) and m-dashes (–) are often used to simulate kireji.

In Basho's time, there were eighteen recognized kireji. Some are still in use in ordinary Japanese. Questions or exclamations (maybe like our '?!') can be expressed with the kireji '–kana' appended to a word. 'Ya' can modulate emphasis the way an English speaker might use a quieter voice, sometimes to soften the message, sometimes to make it harsher. In an online discussion on The Haiku Foundation site, a contributor suggests that in English, certain interjections may be the equivalents of kireji. In this collection, I do not use many interjections but they show up here and there. It is in the 'no' in "zip? no, it does not", the 'what' in "what a mild winter", the 'see' in "see? reaching, dancing", the 'don't it' in "looks like waste, don't it?" and various aaahs and ohs and heys. They are all words that are logically superfluous but make the reader pause. I would even argue that most, maybe all, the repetitions create the same effect.

Technicalities aside, how does kireji heighten the haiku experience? The crack in the bowl, the surprise, punctuation, thought pause, contrast (or juxtaposition, as it often appears) – what do they do for us? I think they serve as a subtle way to invite reflection. Let's take this haiku by Issa

in the middle of a horde
of noisy children –
one tired sparrow
(trans.Hamill)

Perhaps there could be a different kireji instead, but without any the haiku would be a nonsensical, incomplete run-on sentence. The kireji makes sense of the juxtaposition and points to how we can perceive such a seemingly unimportant, everyday, easy-to-overlook occurrence. The small, tired sparrow in the middle of this melee – how frightened and confused it must feel. Will it survive? Maybe not. Will it simply end up as a blob of squashed, dusty feathers trampled under the children's feet? If so, will the children notice? And the children, are they themselves not also sparrows – which hordes are they exposed to? Perhaps the sparrow survives and learns to avoid noisy children. The reader is invited to co-experience, and to contemplate these questions and more. That is the essence of haiku. The kireji is a useful tool in highlighting this essence.

However, in reading across the haiku landscape, I have seen nothing that shows the kireji as essential – at least not in the obvious sense. Even Cohen, who is fond of kireji, does not always use them. For example in this translation of Seibi:

the cold, rainy day
makes these scarecrows
share our human fate

Flawed beauty

Originally, wabi pointed to the loneliness of living in nature. Sabi, in old Japanese the same word as 'rust,' meant 'chill', 'lean' or 'withered.' Today, wabi sabi is often translated as 'flawed beauty.' – Do I create flawed beauty in my haiku? Or only 'flawed?'

"Today John is sad ..... and so, so very lonely ..... he's also chilly."

This shows the 5-7-5 structure, includes loneliness (even melancholy?) as well as 'chill.' But, sadly, it is not a good haiku.

'Not good' is not the same as 'flawed.' What is a flaw? The fly in the ointment, the 3% missing from 100%, a beauty mark, a limp, a missing button? A flaw is a difference noticed on a whole. John's haiku is boring, clichéd, not cohesive, unskillful. It may be flawed, but it is not flawed beauty.

Little is worth noticing in the John haiku. Nothing has been said. I feel no curiosity about why John is sad, lonely or chilly; the poem makes me think of those unfortunate moments when I hurry past a panhandler, unwilling to give money, uninterested in her humanity or her story. If the John haiku were the first haiku I presented to you, you probably would not have wanted to read on.

The following haiku is hopefully more worthy of notice.

You and I may not find garbage delicious. But crows ...

the crow wasn't prepared
but there it sat - all that garbage.
oh my! delicious!

Crows

Crows, by the way, are a special fascination in haiku, not just for me (this book contains only five of my many crow haiku.) One of Basho's most cited haiku is about *karasu*, the Japanese word for raven, crow, or, some say, any black bird.

on a dead
limb squats a crow.
autumn night

(trans. attributed to Kececioglu by Sutiste)

Isn't karasu a wonderfully onomatopoeic word for crow? Karaa, karaa!

On first glance, crows seem unimportant, negligible like the panhandler we pass by, not even of fleeting importance. On second glance, they might simply be a nuisance, a flaw on the city's landscape as they pick through discarded McDonald's wrappings or tap-tap-tap on the roof, disturbing a longed-for Sunday afternoon nap.

Haiku, those tiny little, negligible seventeen syllables, invite us to go deeper. Look at that crow! Pause for a moment to observe it over there by the waste can. Its eyes and body language betray great smarts: the most intelligent of all birds, a species endowed with culture and language. Its black-on-black features and uncompromising arrogance strike as mysterious, perhaps a little disturbing.

From some old place inside arise dim memories of black birds as harbingers of death … long-forgotten dreams … messengers of the gods … the Kwakiutl trickster-cum-creator …

Reflections on Chapter 4 – Not Wabi Sabi: Exclamations, violence, harsh awakenings

Not wabi sabi

Catching with beautiful words the moment of a lone crow sitting on a bare branch may be very wabi sabi, but not so running into a murder of crows: Get the hell out of here! Crows are beautiful, and a nuisance. Barren branches call forth melancholy, and the damnable misery of endless cold, dark days.

> *One element of wabi sabi is mutedness, understatement. Imagine Queen Elizabeth II in her wellingtons, quietly trudging through the forest with her dogs. That is wabi sabi. Now imagine Cher on stage, bright lipstick, made up to the hilt, belting out "Believe". Not wabi sabi.*
>
> *But, what if the flawed, muted beauty of wabi sabi repeats without pause? What if the Queen's forest were endless, never interrupted by a highway or a gaggle of loudmouthed teenage girls? We would be back to the Monopoly Man's ideal park – beautiful, and frozen.*

Beautiful – scary; muted – loud; a quiet forest – a noisy highway.

How I deal with those opposites, or the perception that they are opposites, is similar to the duality of perfection – imperfection. I sense the difference, perceive the pull to one side and sometimes the other, suspect that one end of the pole cannot exist without the other. I feel confusion, frustration, curiosity, anger, helplessness, delight, call them paradoxes, throw up my hands, turn my back, and yet, come back for more.

I want to write 'pure' haiku, adhere to tradition as much as I can. Then I write a haiku. Then I sulk at all rules and ditch them, write another haiku. Then, tentatively, I come back, and stick my nose into my decades-old little *Haiku Harvest* collection, and let myself be touched by these beautiful translations –

hop out of my way
and allow me please to plant bamboo,
mr. toad!

(Chora, trans. Beilensohn/Behn)

I think now, finally, all is well in my poetic world, until the next day. I review a haiku I had written and liked a few weeks ago, wonder where the kireji is, question whether I need it or not, and everything starts all over again.

Life. Life! And Plato

we left him behind,
that sinister man, harper.
cheers and relief!!!

I say that this haiku "fell out of me, uncontrolled, unstructured" – that is exactly how haiku are meant to be written. Yet, how to reconcile what is uncontrolled and spontaneous with haiku's many rules and guidelines? There is the possibility of not calling it a haiku but to me, it is one. We find here, in these short three lines, an example of the old questions: What is art, and what is good art?

In the Western world, one of the earliest records of a response comes from Plato. He quarrels in the Republic: "It is necessary that the good poet, if he is going to make fair poems about the things his poetry concerns, be in possession of knowledge when he makes his poems."

Here I can claim a reasonable measure of understanding. I knew about my relief and Prime Minister Harper's departure in the Canadian election of 2015. As to the alleged sinister nature of the man and the exclamation marks, this takes me into the realm of rhetoric, a technique Plato frowns upon - really, growls at - even more than poetry. I am sure Blyth and other haiku experts would frown as well. One hopes that true to wabi sabi, they would abstain from growling but according to Jane Reichhold, fierce fights were had over such topics.

Plato is suspicious of poetry but condones it when it is inspired by the Muses. But can I prove that the Muses inspired me with this haiku? Inspiration is such a private experience. Plato would say a person using rhetoric simply states a supposed fact ("The Muses have visited me!") and does it in such dramatic fashion that there is no need to prove any of that knowledge that makes for a good poet.

At hand, too, is another justification which Plato may well identify as a rhetorical trick: cherry-picking a respectable theory to agree with my aims. Here, I could use philosopher Noel Carroll's definition of art: "... created by an artist in an artistic context with a recognized and live artistic motivation, and as a result of being so created, it resembles at least one acknowledged artwork."

If that is the case: I am a writer, have written this poem in the context of my haiku writing, and it looks haiku-ish. See - we have a work of art!

Folk Art, and a Paradox

To a large degree I stand with Plato when it comes to the Harper haiku. It is not a particularly 'good' haiku in an abstract aesthetic sense; it is unlikely to appear in a serious anthology of Canadian haiku. It brings to mind, though, a sense of folk art: happy good times at barn dances, or the peasant art found in European churches, painted by grateful mothers, brothers and friends whose prayers to the Saints have been answered. The music may not be entirely in tune, and the drawings are often clumsy but it all looks and feels good.

Just like a haiku, this art bypasses the aesthetics of the intellect, reaching directly into the aesthetics of the heart, and the heart responds, Yes! Yes, this music makes me dance! Yes, these paintings talk to my soul; and yes, this is how, I, too, respond to Harper being gone.

In these surroundings the harlot-red lipstick of the exclamation marks takes on a different hue. It is no longer an aesthetic faux pas. Paradoxically, there is nothing muted or desolate about this little poem about Harper, which does not make it wabi-sabi. But because there is something norm-like about a wabi-sabi feel in haiku, this haiku fulfills exactly one idea put forth by wabi-sabi authority Leonard Koren: "Wabi sabi = the aesthetic other [which] offers contrast with, and differentiation from, the dominant aesthetic convention."

Not Haiku? Senryu – Haiku About People

Some haiku experts make a distinction between haiku and senryu. Haiku, they say, are about nature, senryu about people. Haiku often have a somewhat serious tone; senryu can be more humorous. Senryu can speak directly to emotions, and make no bones about it. The Harper haiku is one stark example; so is this:

addiction: lust "must"
never "maybe" or "later"
and wants THIS and NOW

The humour is often sarcastic; here sarcasm serves as a tool to point out a stongly felt, ugly truth. Would it be too far-fetched to assert a similarity between an ugly truth and flawed beauty? Is it wabi-sabi? Not? One thing for sure, it is about human nature. Interesting, too, how the gentle this-here-now of drawing a haiku-picture of the moment contorts into a This! Now!

Japanese haiku writers of the last 120 years observed the harshness of the human experience. Ueda's outstanding anthology, tracing haiku poetry since Shiki's invention of the term 'haiku' in 1892, gives many such examples, without ever, to my knowledge, referring to the term senryu. Here is Tomizawa Kakio's bitter exclamation, in Ueda's translation:

good will?
how far do the rings
of zeros extend?

Bitterness moves on to violence in what I wrote here:

really. believe me.
yes, this is for your own good.
WHACK! and one more blow

From personal violence on to the public violence of war:

a machine gun –
in the middle of the forehead
red blossoms bloom
(Sanki, trans. Ueda)

Reflections on Chapter 5 – This. No More.

This.

The word 'this' shows up more in this book than in anything else I have written. Normally an inconspicuous word (a 'demonstrative,' grammatically speaking) it suddenly takes on significance – like the everyday crows, like the negligible little three-line haiku.

If we take our time and accept the word 'this' as one complete statement, it is possible, as Christopher Ives states, to intuitively know that "even though there is no grammatical subject or object, there already is something self-evident to the speaker and listener." (It is not unusual to accept one word as a statement, for example, when someone says, "uh-oh," so the lack of subject and object or the shortness should not be a problem.)

Imagine we are going for a walk and come to stand under an old oak tree. Then I point and say, "This is an oak." The moment you hear these words, your experience is already limited. You may recall that an oak is a member of a specific species, which is a leaf-bearing tree, which belongs to the kingdom of plants, and so on. You are aware, on a subconscious but certain level, that "this is an oak" also indicates what it is not. It is not a maple tree, nor is it a puppy, a rock concert or a cry for help. Often in life, we would be lost without these distinctions, without our intellect automatically going into such analytical procedure.

However ... we're on a walk! We're standing under a tree! Perhaps it would be much more enjoyable, and a more profound experience, if we grasped this oak, this one right here, in its totality. That totality is so immense that analysis can never fully embrace it; so, paradoxically, we might as well confine ourselves. To seventeen syllables.

Or maybe just one word: This.

> *... this watching, tasting, listening, feeling, smelling, touching, thinking, this doing and not-doing, this glancing at a few words just is. And you don't have to worry that it will go on is-ing forever because any second now the sun will move, the tea cup will empty.*

" 'This' indicates only that which has extinguished all forms, the whole to which no name can be affixed," wrote Christopher Ives, in an article about one of the most venerated Zen texts, *Hisamatsu's Talks on Linji.* Contemplating 'that which has extinguished all forms' is too much – or too little? – for most of us. Soon this nameless suchness, this 'is-ing' dissipates and moves back into ordinary perception.

There is not a single haiku I wrote that comes close to directly expressing 'this' well. Yet I continue.

bent from old old age
this gnarly oak lives on -
a big bird house

The experience of the oak has already shrunk by focusing on characteristics such as old, gnarly, probably tough (it lives on), and the image of a bird house. I can only hope that this poetic focus leads away from purely intellectual analysis and opens up a vista of more than what is presented.

There is one haiku I wrote that at least somewhat approximates the big 'this'. Originally its allusion to a familiar zen story seemed too cliché for me to include it in this selection. But here it is:

unleashed from my self,
my small, ego self, i'm free!
this strawb'ry, how sweet ...

Some haiku in this chapter, while not expressly using the word 'this,' still come close to the sentiment of only presenting an image, without evaluating, adding concepts, or making obvious associations.

winter sunlight
shining down, softly, on my
neighbour's white house

There is a little flavour of evaluation in the word 'softly' but perhaps it can be forgiven, for sun shining on a white house could evoke a more glaring light, ill-suited to capturing the gentleness of the moment that produced this haiku.

Images – pictorial?

The 'winter sunlight' haiku is one of twenty-three that fell into a category I named 'image/visual' – poems with a strong visual element. Before I delved more deeply into the haiku world, I had a notion that good haiku were about visual images. As I read and reflected more I realized this might be a misconception. I open Henderson's *Haiku In English* on a random page and find Issa:

a dewdrop fades away:
it's dirty, this world, and in it
there's no place for me

(tsuru chiru ya musai kono yo ni yo nashi to)

The first line shows an image but the whole of it is not an image. If this were not a haiku, most readers would assume the fading dewdrop to be a metaphor. Knowing how haiku are written, one could assume, however, that seeing the dewdrop fade came first, followed by this thought of loneliness. Even that is not entirely clear – Issa wrote this haiku after the death of his baby daughter. It is not difficult to imagine her as a dewdrop. A different translation, by Lanoue, offers even less visual imagery:

dewdrops scatter--
done with this crappy
world

Let's look at two more Japanese haiku:

i love the rest of my life
though it is transitory
like a light azure morning glory

(Fusei, trans. Miura)

in the coolness
of the empty sixth-month sky...
the cuckoo's cry.

(Shiki; trans. Beichman)

In the first, the visual image is used metaphorically, in the second there is no picture at all. The latter, unlike the preceding two, is all about a sense-image, but is not focusing on anything visual.

What about pictures in non-Japanese haiku? Here are three poems selected at random from another book entitled *Haiku In English*, an authoritative collection compiled by Jim Kacian, Philip Rowland and Allan Burns:

ants out of a hole -
when did i stop playing
the red toy piano?

(Fay Aoyagi)

indian summer.
even a small affection
has its urgency.

(Guenter Klinger)

photos of her father
in enemy uniform -
the taste of almonds

(Sandra Simpson)

None of these poems are as stringently visual as the following, which I used to judge as one of my better haiku, precisely because of the pure visuals:

twelve broken lanterns
on a rainy, slippery bridge:
soft-light quiver

It is possible that this focus on the visual is a beginner's attitude (I have only seriously dabbled in haiku for ten years.) In his section on writing and teaching haiku, Henderson refers to visual haiku as 'objective' or 'pictorial,' but also mentions that children find it much easier to write such haiku; adults find them too elementary.

Let us not forget, too, that we live in a visual culture, and that the human visual sense takes up vast amounts of space in the brain – probably the reason we call what we make up in our heads images. We 'imagine' much more than the visual: ideas, sounds, emotions, memories, but all of it is collected in a concept that points to the visual. In German the word is more kinesthetic: vorstellen, literally to stand before, but meaning to stand something or someone before one's (inner) eye.

Perhaps I was influenced by the fact that two of the 'four pillars' of haiku, Basho and Buson, were painters. (The other two pillars are Issa and Shiki.) Basho and Buson created haiga, paintings with a haiku done in calligraphy.

The Buson scroll here reads:

year ending –
day ending, too, for
a charcoal peddler

(trans. Shimizu)

Both the haiku and the painting stand well on their own but take on a more profound meaning when combined, suggesting Henderson's idea about growth: the more one contemplates this work of art, the more one penetrates and understands.

Haiga is alive and well, including in English. Here is one from a haiga workshop at the Asian Art Museum in San Francisco in 2011 (artist unknown) that captured my eye.

the green leafed wind
a pure amateur scholar
above worldly concerns

Notice the 'amateur scholar.' Possibly, the workshop facilitators referred to the scholar amateur movement in Chinese and Japanese painting which had a strong influence on Buson. Called *wenren hua* in China and *bunjinga* or *nanga* in Japan, it was a style of painting created by well educated, scholarly artists who were untrained in the exacting skill of representational techniques. The decorative and supposedly superficial nature of traditional Chinese and Japanese art was shunned in favour of spontaneous, heartfelt expressions designed to show the essence of what the artists saw before them. This attitude towards painting resembles the philosophy underlying haiku; no wonder people like Buson and Basho naturally took to haiga.

Reflections on Chapter 6 – A Bag Full

Chaos, accidents and magic

In this chapter, I tried to make a haiku more orderly but then

> *"... it doesn't sound like a haiku and is boring and pointless." Take out the chaos and that element of the almost-accidental we find in most haiku, and the magic disappears.*

What a fascinating paradox. On one hand, dozens of rules rake with sharp tines through the landscape of haiku, while on the other, there is a need to be spontaneous.

Heading this section 'chaos, accident and magic' seems provocative – do these words belong in a world born of a culture like the Japanese, with its love for structure and harmony? Yasuda says a haiku should be a "unified, well ordered whole." But as we saw in Chapter 5, there are many ways to order anything. Also, how does order come about? Is it created, is it imposed, does it emerge? Let's look at this with the example of a few more randomly selected haiku:

the grassy lawn:
amid the shimmering heat waves
a dog's dream

(Soseki, trans. Ueda)

That this poem came up in a random selection is in itself an exercise of chaos and order. It turns out that the shimmering heat waves are *kagerou*, a word that in Japanese also stands "as a metaphor for something evanescent, insubstantial or unreal." This points to chaos.

'Chaos' is often used to describe a mass of matter that appears jumbled, random, unorganized. 'Appears' – that may be the important word. A dog's dream, kagerou as it is on that jumble of grass blades, would appear to most humans as jumbled and unorganized. On closer inspection, though, some order can detected, even if it is just the fact that certain things are most likely absent from a canine's dream world. It is not too far fetched to assume that the dog does not dream of kayaking in Hawaii, of climbing up abstract-looking staircases leading to nowhere or of complicated formulae in chaos theory mathematics, all of which have occurred in my very human dreams. Chaos is often relative to the observer; just think of the proverbial messy office that looks hopelessly chaotic to a new person entering, when its regular occupant can locate a single piece of paper within seconds, two inches down on the blue pile beside the wastepaper basket.

In this poem, chaos shows up as kagerou but in a way that makes sense to the human mind: it is easy to imagine a snoozing mutt there on that summer lawn. Sense-making itself is an act of creating order. Then sometimes there is randomness, like in the choosing of this haiku, but it turns out to fit exactly: we talk about chaos and haiku, and what appears at random? A haiku about something with no discernible order.

Magic and the accidental are also present. Kagerou is quintessentially magic. Dreams may not be accidental per se but they are also rarely deliberate; I doubt our dog here is an expert in lucid dreaming.

Chaos, accident and magic are starkly evident in a haiku from the Basho section in Carl Johnson's *Classical Japanese Database*:

the autumn wind
is my lament.
move with it, gravemound!

(my adaptation, inspired by Miyamori)

This poem was written on the occasion of visiting a student, only to find him dead and buried. I am particularly touched by "move with it, gravemound!" a rageful, helpless attempt at magic.

Finally, a recent English-language haiku, a runner-up from the 2012 Haiku Foundation awards:

august night?—
kisses she learned
from a book

(Glenn G. Coats)

Once again, we find magic – that of the night, and of the first kiss. How accidental it is we do not know, but we can just imagine the jumble in a young girl's thoughts and emotions as she tries to apply her book learning in those last days of summer.

Magic, chaos, the accidental and spontaneous are abundant in any art form but it is surprising how easily they can be pinpointed in a literary realm that has as many boundaries and constrictions as haiku.

Meaning and interpretation

> *Without that magic, we can slip into interpretation, rather than the quietly reflective, contemplative mode so much better suited to haiku. We might poke and prod and look for certainty about what 'it' is, for example, or what is 'meant' by the poem.*
>
> *Like the crumbs in the old purse and the long-forgotten reason why that teddy bear came to hang from the keychain, the haiku's meaning might not be easy to decipher, and there may be more than one meaning.*

I have a difficult relationship with meaning. First, it is a hard concept to pin down. A philosophy professor once told us to stay away from the term; it was so woolly, he thought, that we would just get hopelessly entangled. Too many questions arise. Is meaning about what the speaker/writer intends to say? What the reader/listener makes of it? What can be looked up in a reference, be it Webster's, an Atlas or a dream dictionary?

There is a second problem: how important is meaning and what place does it have? For some types of things the question of meaning is nonsensical (meaningless, so to say). When we walk into a forest, we don't stop and ask, "What is the meaning of this tree?" In other situations, meaning is highly important, for example when someone needs to know the meaning of a diagnosis of multiple sclerosis. In the latter, we are looking for the implications (what do we need to do now?) and perhaps a translation (what do those words mean in plain English?) and illustration (what happens in the body when someone has multiple sclerosis?) We may also be looking for reasons (why did this happen?) or a purpose (will suffering make me a better person?)

So I have difficulty with meaning. It is part of the human condition that we feel better if we can control things, and thinking – correctly or incorrectly – that we understand the meaning, purpose or reason of those things helps us feel in control. When something new comes along, we have a need to control it by knowing more about it. This makes sense with an illness. How much sense does it make for a poem, or any work of art?

As a creative, I have lived all my life among art-makers, from playwrights to violinists, from sculptors to poets and painters, many of them abstract and experimental. With this experience, I lack the perspective of being exclusively on the side of the audience. This makes me both curious and skittish. The skittish part of me suspects that the audience wants to control a piece of art by grasping – yes, grasping – its meaning. In some of my nightmarish visions I see it as leaving claw marks of superficial understanding ... and in my more compassionate and rational moments it is I who seeks to understand: what does the audience need when it keeps pressing for meaning and reasons and explanations?

"Please bring me my poems cooked medium rare," says Charles Trumbull in his essay *Meaning in Haiku* in *Frogpond,* the Haiku Society of America journal. He claims poems are vehicles for transmitting meaning but I cannot necessarily agree. Many years ago I used a similar metaphor for language in general; language, too, is much more than transportation units shuttling superficial meaning back and forth, like some sort of courier service of understanding. Like all forms of art, language and poetry always have a synesthetic quality – the written word is not just scribbles. It is music and dance in its rhythm, and shape (remember the beautiful haiga calligraphy!) It is the feeling of lips and tongue and throat. It is colour in the images it evokes. Beyond that, it is the ungraspable resonance, that feeling when a word, phrase, or image falls into the fertile ground of the reader's mind-heart-body-soul and a song arises, composed of the writer's call and the reader's response.

up on the 12th floor
hair black, voice soft as velvet
echo is her name

Using Turnbull's steak metaphor, this haiku would probably be blue, nay, completely raw. It is a very private poem. Echo was the name of the first Korean person I ever met. Everything about her fascinated little seven-year-old me: her long black hair, her accent, the way she made rice, how she met her husband, the fact they lived high, high, high up on the 12th floor ... but how can readers know that? They cannot. And yet, something made me pick this haiku out of hundreds of others and present it to you, in the unexplainable, irrational, hopeful conviction that something will be touched in you when you read it.

But really, how do I know? I don't. It's easy, though, to fall prey to thinking I do. As I believe Trumbull did here: "There can't be much doubt about the warmth of his lady friend's feelings in Marsh Muirhead's senryu,"

her cold martini
the olive
looks at me

There may not be much doubt among some readers, but I certainly had quite a bit of it. I did not see any warmth or even flirtation, if that's what Trumbull was referring to. This is a great illustration of the fickleness of meaning. Trumbull was so sure of the clarity of a meaning full of appreciation, yet for me this martini piece remains cloudy, its olive eyeing me with everything from mockery to curiosity to a cold scientific stare.

Juxtaposition and Relationship

Before we close this bag of haiku, let us briefly talk about juxtaposition, something discussed frequently in the haiku literature. To juxtapose literally translates as 'to put side by side;' often it is used for comparison or contrast. Trumbull sees juxtaposition as "perhaps the most important source of meaning in haiku."

Words like juxtaposition, contrast and comparison put me in mind of college essays, involving somewhat facile notions of persuasion, performance and teaching. But I do resonate with the idea of putting things side by side, and with the idea of relationship. "Haiku," says Jim Kacian, "are always about relationship." While I flinch at the 'always,' I find the equality implied in the concept of relationship more to my liking than the feeling of evaluation that comes from contrasting and comparing. Choosing one of my haiku at random:

i misunderstand
these winter days when i stay
huddled in my cave

we immediately find an element of evaluation in the word 'misunderstand.' Contrast, too: the cold outside and the desire to stay protected from it. And relationship: want it or not, I am confronted with, have to deal with the reality of weather, even if it is just hiding from it.

The following shows very little contrast or comparison:

slow rain on tired
tulips; waxing moon rising.
clouds make me sleepy.

I asked a few people to tell me their opinions and reactions to this haiku, perhaps what they thought it might mean, if anything. Two people saw contrast, others did not mention it. But everyone captured elements of the essence of what I experienced when I wrote this haiku. Establishing a mutual understanding of this essence is far more satisfying and interesting than conveying any meaning. The relationship, then, exists not only within the haiku (between the rain and the tulips, for example,) but also between the writer and the reader.

Apart from the essence, the fact about the tired tulips was that they were at the end of their bloom. One could make a case that there is contrast between a fading tulip and a waxing moon. I would have been pleased if someone had pointed that out. Not because it would prove that I had been successful in making them 'get' a meaning, but for the same reason that I am pleased that people shared their reactions. None of them would have been mine; at the same time none of them shocked or surprised me. But if they had, I hope I would reply, 'how interesting!' rather than become concerned that I was misunderstood. "Once your story is out in the open the interpretation you wrote is no longer the only one, nor is it the definitive one. That's one of the reasons art is so amazing," says the blogger Ceilidh. How true.

A bag not full yet

In the bag of this chapter you find codependence, Bob Marley, yawns, fingertips, staring, Old Smith, blood, comrades, bras, warm socks, a teddy bear, up North, dreams and blue faces. No rhyme. No reason. Make your own sense of it. Put it into your bag. Hang a haiku from your keychain.

Better yet, write your own haiku (or poem, or story.) Everything you have read in this book so far are just ideas, plays with words, opinions. Don't take them too seriously; don't take me too seriously. I hope I have entertained you, helped you spend a few minutes here and there in an engaging way – nothing I presented is absolute.

Not only does the last chapter of Part I contain a grab-bag of poems; the whole book is a grab-bag of ideas about haiku. None of these should be so much of an authority as to hold you back from enjoying haiku just the way you want to, or writing haiku in any fashion you desire.

I don't say this carelessly, in an effort to be nice or naively inclusive. I didn't say it at the beginning of this book, I say it at the end, after you have been exposed to a goodly amount of all the structures and strictures surrounding and permeating the enjoyment of haiku. I say it as someone who put care into following the rules of the English language – but in a way that works for me. I say it as someone with a solid understanding of creative and non-fiction writing, and who then flaunts convention, breaks the fourth wall by talking to you directly. I am saying this as a non-Japanese writer who creates poetry that still has not cut its umbilical cord to the land of Nippon. Structure and rules are useful, but as a trellis for growth, not a box to contain. This bag of haiku is not closed; it's open and roomy, for you and for me.

It is a specific bag. In it, so far, are mostly rather tame and conventional haiku. But there is so much more, for you and for me to explore.

Here is a taste from a few contemporary haiku collections.:

window . . . to window . . . and back . . . the cat

(Celia Stuart-Powles)

redwood silence from a different century

(Cherie Hunter Day)

the answer is yes no
yes breaking waves

(Robert Epstein)

left
home
less
scare
crow
chimney

(Peter Newton)

And on!

Write haiku! Use the blank pages at the end of this book. Or write in the margins of this one.

Remember the rules ... or defy them altogether.

Write rule-free haiku that:

Boast and exaggerate / Wear as many rings on the finger pointing to the moon as can be crammed into 17 (or 25 or 7) syllables / Occur in the most unnatural place imaginable

Use obscure, academic language / Incorporate as many ambiguous syllables as possible ("water," "mirror") / Sparkle and glitter

Talk about exotic animals / Are as artistic as dishwasher instruction / Leave no question open

Contain obvious clichés / Rhyme about the sameness of identical twins / Omit all references to the senses

Want to haiku?
Here's your invitation.
All these blank pages …

You can also tweet! If you use the hashtag #haikubag, I and other readers of this book will see it. I tweet at @moritherapy

Glossary

Amidha Buddha - The Buddha of Pure Land (Shin) Buddhism. On all accounts, this is not a historical figure but a deified symbol of wisdom, compassion and enlightenment

Bodhisattvas - Enlightened beings who have made a vow not to enter nirvana until every last sentient being is free from suffering. On some accounts, also persons who strive in that direction

Bunjinga, also called Nanga - Paintings created by Chinese intellectuals/scholars not formally trained in the visual arts

Chinpunkan (or chinpunkanpun) - Gibberish

Haiga - Paintings that combine visual elements, traditionally drawing and calligraphy, with the aesthetics found in haiku/haikai

Haikai - A Chinese character/word standing for "comical" or "not serious"; also, short form for haikai no renga

Haikai no renga - Japanese linked verse that emerged in the Edo period, around 1600. "Renga" were composed serially by poets right on the spot, a popular pastime in medieval times in China and later also Japan. The haikai no renga that started in the Edo period were "not serious" verses, typically composed by poets of a social status lower than traditional renga poets. They also comprised a wider range of topics than the imperially sanctioned ones in traditional renga.

Harusame - Soft spring rain; a kigo (season word)

Hokku - The starting verse of haikai no renga, usually composed by a senior poet. Haiku evolved from hokku

Kagerou - A metaphor for something evanescent, insubstantial or unreal

Kaizen - A practice of continuous improvement, started in post-WWII Japan. The word itself means "change for the better"

Kanzeon (Kuanyin, Guanyin, etc.) -A female bodhisattva, sometimes referred to as 'Goddess of Mercy.'

Kigo -A word symbolizing the season in which a haiku takes place

Kireji - A "cutting word" indicating the point between one part of a haiku and another

Koan - A riddle used in zen teachings which cannot be solved with analytical means

Kwakiutl (Kwakwaka'wakw) - A Canadian Indigenous territory at the north end of Vancouver Island and adjacent mainland

On - A "beat" in a Japanese word, similar to a syllable in the English

Pure Land Buddhism - A form of Buddhism marked by calling on Amida Buddha to attain enlightenment

Raku - A type of Japanese pottery

Renga - See haikai no renga

Sabi - See wabi sabi

Senryu - A type of haiku that focuses on the human condition, often employing humour or sarcasm

Shin Buddhism - A form of Pure Land Buddhism, the most frequently practiced Buddhism in Japan

Twaiku - Haiku composed on/for Twitter

Wabi sabi - Originally, wabi pointed to the loneliness of living in nature. Sabi, refers to 'chill', 'lean' or 'withered.' Today, wabi sabi is often translated as 'flawed beauty.'

Waka - A Japanese poetic form still practiced today but preceding haiku. It has thirty-one syllables (five lines of 5/7/5/7/7 syllables)

Wenren - See Bunjinga

Yugen - A subtle, mysterious profundity pointing to the essence of a thing

Zazen - The practice of sitting in zen meditation

Bibliography

Adajian, Thomas: *The Definition of Art* (The Stanford Encyclopedia of Philosophy (Summer 2016 Edition), Edward N. Zalta (ed.), referring to Carroll, Noel, 1993, "Historical Narratives and the Philosophy of Art", The Journal of Aesthetics and Art Criticism, 51(3):313–26. Available online at http://plato.stanford.edu/archives/sum2016/entries/art-definition/

Bashô, Matsuo; Kececioglu, John (trans.), attributed by Sütiste, Elin (2001): A Crow on a Bare Branch. A comparison of Matsuo Bashô's haiku "Kare-eda-ni…" and its English translations. In *Studia Humaniora Tartuensia* (2), B.1.1-21.

Bashô, Matsuo, Miyamori, Asataro (trans.) In *Matsuo Basho: WKD Archives*. Available at https://www.facebook.com/MatsuoBashoWkdArchives/posts/1198051348697785

Beichman, Janine (1986): Masaoka Shiki. Tokyo: Kodansha International

Beilenson, Peter & Behn, Harry (1962): Haiku harvest. Japanese haiku, series IV. Mt. Vernon New York: Peter Pauper.

Beckett, Samuel (1984): Worstward Ho. New York: Grove Press

Blyth, R. H. (1981): Haiku. vol 2, Spring. Tokyo: Hokuseido Press.

Buson, Yosa; Shimizu, Kuniharu (trans.) (2015): Yosa Buson exhibition in Tenri. Available online at http://seehaikuhere.blogspot.ca/2015/10/an-exhibition-on-yosa-buson-is-going-on.html. (Same reference for the image)

Ceilidh (2012): Comment on Cassandra Clare Talks about Rape Culture and a Publisher Dies. Available at http://ohnotheydidnt.livejournal.com/69160890.html#ixzz4bKi7XtAW,

Chula, Margaret (2010): Harmony: Poetry and a Bowl of Tea. Available online at http://margaretchula.blogspot.ca/2010_04_01_archive.html

Cohen, William Howard (compiler) (1972): To walk in seasons. An introduction to Haiku. S.l.: Tuttle.

Dai, Qun (2016) Chinese and Japanese Literati Painting: Analysis and Contrasts in Japanese Bunjinga Paintings. In Bard College Digital Commons, 2016 Bard Undergraduate Senior Projects. Available at http://digitalcommons.bard.edu/cgi/viewcontent.cgi?article=1064&context=senproj_s2016

Epstein, Robert (2015): In The Heron's Nest. December 2015, Vol XVII, No 4: December 2015. Available at http://www.theheronsnest.com/December2015/haiku-p5.html,

Gilbert, Richard; Yoneoka, Judy (2000): From 5-7-5 to 8-8-8: An Investigation of Japanese Haiku Metrics and Implications for English Haiku. In Language Issues: Journal of the Foreign Language Education Center March 2000, No.1. Available online at http://terebess.hu/english/haiku/total2.html,

Hackett, James W. (2002): Reflections. In World Haiku Review 2-1. Available online at https://whrarchives.wordpress.com/2013/02/19/reflections/

Henderson, Harold Gould (Ed.) (1958): An introduction to haiku. An anthology of poems and poets from Basho to Shiki. Garden City N.Y.: Doubleday (Doubleday anchor books).

Henderson, Harold Gould (1967): Haiku in English. Rutland, Vt., & Tokyo, printed in Japan: Charles E. Tuttle Co.

Higginson, William J.; Harter, Penny (1985): The haiku handbook. How to write, teach, and appreciate haiku, Tokyo, London: Kodansha International. Available online at http://www.loc.gov/catdir/enhancements/fy1008/2009036628-b.html,

Hisamatsu, Shinichi; Ives, Christopher; Tokiwa, Gishin (2002): Critical sermons of the Zen tradition. Hisamatsu's talks on Linji / translated and edited by Christopher Ives and Tokiwa Gishin. Basingstoke: Palgrave Macmillan.

Hunter-Day, Cherie (2015): In The Heron's Nest Reader's Choice Award. 2015. Available at http://www.theheronsnest.com/awards/awards_2015.html

Inahata, Teiko (n.d.); Greves, Gabi (ed, 2007): In: *Introducing Haiku Poets and Topics*. Available at https://wkd-haikutopics.blogspot.ca/2007/02/haiku-definitions.html

Issa, Kobayashi; Hamill, Sam (trans.) (1997): The spring of my life. And selected haiku. 1st ed. Boston: Shambhala; Distributed in the U.S. by Random House.

Issa, Kobayashi; Lanoue, David G. (trans.) (2013): Haiku of Kobayashi Issa. Available online at http://haikuguy.com/issa

Johnson, Carl. Classical Japanese Database. Available at http://www.carlsensei.com/classical/index.php/

Kacian, Jim; Rowland, Philip; Burns, Allan (2013): Haiku in English. The first hundred years. First edition. New York, London: W.W. Norton & Company.

Kerouac, Jack (1986, 1959): American haikus. New Jersey: Caliban.

Klabund; Bogner, Ralf. G. et al (eds.) (2017): Werke in acht Baenden. Berlin: Elfenbein Verlag

Koren, Leonard (2008, 1994): Wabi-sabi for artists, designers, poets & philosophers. Point Reyes: Imperfect Pub.

Lorin (2011): kireji. Available online at http://www.thehaikufoundation.org/forum_sm/index.php?topic=717.msg11401#msg11401

Millard, Maggie (2015): 10 Haikus About Continuous Improvement. Available online at https://blog.kainexus.com/continuous-improvement/best-practices-for-continuous-improvement/10-haikus

Miura, Yuzuru (1991): Classic haiku. A master's selection / selected and translated by Yuzuru Miura. Boston: Tuttle Pub

Muirhead, Marsh (2008): In Modern Haiku 39:2 (Summer 2008).

Newton, Peter (2015): In Bones - journal for contemporary haiku 2015, November, Vol 8, available at http://www.bonesjournal.com/no8/bones8.pdf

Plato; Bloom, Allan (1991): The Republic of Plato. 2nd ed. New York: Basic Books.

Powell, Richard R. (2005): Wabi sabi simple. Create beauty, value imperfection, live deeply. Avon, Mass.: Adams Media.

Reichhold, Jane (2002): Writing and enjoying haiku. A hands-on guide. Tokyo, London: Kodansha International.

Shirane, Haruo (2008): Beyond the Haiku Moment: Basho, Buson and Modern Haiku Myths. In Simply Haiku: A Quarterly Journal of Japanese Short Form Poetry. Autumn 2008, vol 6 no 3. Available online at http://simplyhaiku.com/SHv6n3/reprints/Shirane.html

Stuart-Prowles, Celia: In 2016 Harold G. Henderson Haiku Awards. Available at http://www.hsa-haiku.org/hendersonawards/henderson-judges2016.htm

Trumbull, Charles (2012): Meaning in Haiku. In Frogpond. 2012, vol 35.3. Available at http://www.hsa-haiku.org/frogpond/2012-issue35-3/essay.html

Ueda, M. (1976): Modern Japanese Haiku. An anthology. S.l.: Univ. of Toronto Press.

Wakan, Naomi (1997, ©1993): Haiku. One breath poetry. 1st American ed. Torrance, CA: Heian.

Unknown Artist (2011): Haiga created during Workshop: Japanese Haiku Painting (Haiga) by Michael Hofmann and Patricia J. Machmiller at the Asian Art Museum, San Francisco, on September 24, 2011. Available under Creative Commons at http://tinyurl.com/mesm9yf

Wehrli, Ursus (2003): Tidying up art. Munich, London: Prestel.

Yasuda, Kenneth (1957, 2000 printing): The Japanese haiku, its essential nature, history, and possibilities in English, with selected examples. Boston: Tuttle Pub.

Acknowledgements

It takes a village to write a book. Such a solitary act and yet, it cannot be done alone. I thank my soul-brother Nikolai and my mother, both of whom have passed on but who, in my heart, were the ones to whom I whispered many of these words as I wrote them. My husband Glenn, who spoke to me of music and rhythm in poetry, and whose Japanese ancestry was always somewhere in the background. My daughter Tova, whose gentle spirit flowed beside me through the production of this book. My daughter Mindemoya, whose passion and loyalty spurn me on. My two writing groups, and particularly Margo, Brant and Mario, who put effort into supporting me. All the writers who came before me! Please leaf through the bibliography – every single work there is a treasure. Specifically, Kerouac, Ueda, Wakan and Higginson stand, giant-like, behind me, and I imagine them nodding with benevolence at my imperfect attempts. This book probably would not have happened without Twitter. @baffled, who runs a daily Haiku Challenge, was very much an inspiration. Arianna, Lorna, Monica, Lisa, Benjamin, Katana Leigh, Jen, and Tara were among the forty-odd people who participated in a survey to find out what people liked in haiku. My greatest thanks, though, go to my "book midwife," friend, and wise woman Carol Sill, who, through patient encouragement, not to mention editing and layout magic, made this book the beautiful thing you hold in your hands.

About the Author

Isabella Mori is a mother, grandmother, wife, friend, sister. She also writes: poetry, novels, short stories and non-fiction, and has published a book of poetry, *isabella mori's tea table book*. She lives in Vancouver, Canada, in a way-too-big house, enjoys being surrounded by houseplants, flowers and trees, and takes long, long walks. She grew up in Germany in a wonderfully chaotic artists' household and spent some time in the UK, Paraguay and Chile. Isabella has a Masters Degree in Education and works in the mental health/addiction field.

Made in the USA
Middletown, DE
18 March 2024

51277369R00076